LEADERSHIP
ENERGY
$(E=mc^2)$

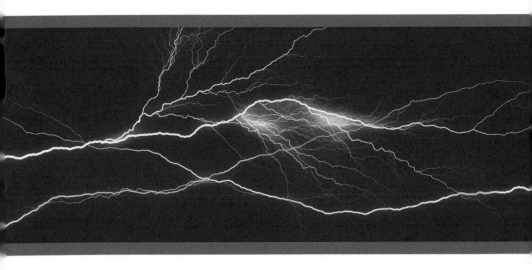

A High-Velocity Formula to Energize Your Team, Customers and Profits

DAVID COTTRELL

LEADERSHIP ENERGY
$(E=mc^2)$

A High-Velocity Formula to Energize Your Team, Customers and Profits

CornerStone Leadership Institute
P.O. Box 764087
Dallas, TX 75376
888.789.LEAD

Printed in the United States of America
ISBN: 978-0-9798009-3-1

Credits

Contributing Writer	Alice Adams, Austin, TX
Copy Editor	Juli Baldwin, The Baldwin Group, Dallas, TX Juli@BaldwinGrp.com
Proofreader	Kathleen Green, Positively Proofed, Plano, TX info@PositivelyProofed.com
Design, art direction, and production	Melissa Monogue, Back Porch Creative, Plano, TX info@BackPorchCreative.com

CONTENTS

gratis

118827

Part One:

The Power of Energy

Introduction

The Formula – $E=mc^2$

Why Energy Leaks Occur

Mass: Building the Right Organization

INTRODUCTION

Not everything that counts can be counted,
and not everything that can be counted counts.

– Sign hanging in Einstein's office at Princeton

Albert Einstein's formula, **E=mc²**, has been called the most celebrated equation of all time. Breathtaking in its simplicity yet revolutionary in its impact, his formula fundamentally transformed scientific thinking about the universe.

Einstein's equation, which directly evolved from his work on the theory of special relativity, challenged well-established theories about mass and energy. Up until 1905, when Einstein developed his theory, scientists believed that mass and energy were two different things. Einstein was the first to propose the radical idea that mass and energy are two forms of the *same* thing, and that neither appears without the other.

Einstein's theory was so revolutionary at the time that there was no way to verify it – and in fact, another 25 years would pass before anyone *could* prove it. Years later, his deceptively simple formula laid the groundwork for the development of both nuclear energy and nuclear weapons. In many ways, Einstein's theory changed the course of human history. Talk about a formula that's had a powerful impact!

Leadership Energy...E=mc² borrows some principles of Einstein's famous theory about mass and energy in the universe, and applies them to help explain the energy found in successful, high-achieving organizations. Like Einstein's formula, the **Leadership Energy** formula is based on simple principles. But don't let its simplicity fool you. In combination with the accompanying straightforward techniques, the **Leadership Energy** formula has the power to transform your organization.

First, though, let's address the question that's probably on your mind: What is organizational energy, anyway?

Admittedly, organizational energy is one of those concepts that's difficult to define and impossible to measure. But there's no denying that organizational energy is a powerful force that fuels the success of many high-achieving organizations.

In trying to define organizational energy, perhaps it's useful to first define what it's *not*. Organizational energy is *not* just short-term enthusiasm for the latest corporate program-of-the-month, and it is *not* just a week-long buzz that follows an executive weekend retreat. Although emotions like excitement and enthusiasm are often a byproduct, organizational energy itself is grounded in something much deeper — a solid commitment to an organization, its mission and values, and an unshakable desire to propel the organization to achieve bigger and better things.

The potential for energy resides in every employee, every team, and every department within an organization. But tapping into and releasing that energy is a task for an organization's leaders. And once the energy has been released, the leaders must then find a way to focus that energy to achieve the organization's goals.

Leadership Energy contains all the practical tools and techniques you need to harness the energy of your organization and move it to higher levels of achievement.

And the best part? You don't have to be an Einstein to learn and apply its principles. This book will provide you with the knowledge required to energize your team, your customers and your profits.

Read, enjoy and apply our leadership version of $E=mc^2$.

CHAPTER ONE

THE FORMULA

$E = mc^2$

Let's begin with a more detailed look at Einstein's famous formula, **E=mc²**, and an assessment of each element.

In this equation, which is known as Einstein's theory of special relativity:

E represents **energy**

m represents **mass**

c^2 represents **the square of the speed of light in a vacuum**

In its simplest non-mathematical form, Einstein's equation states that energy and mass are equivalent and interchangeable – two different forms of the same thing.

When you think about this amazing concept you start to appreciate Einstein's genius. According to Einstein, every object – a book, a lawn chair, a can of tuna – is really a reservoir of energy just waiting to be unlocked. But we can unlock the energy of mass *only* by multiplying it by the square of the speed of light. Given that the speed of light is such an enormous number (670 million mph) and its square is even more enormous, you start to realize that you don't need much mass to produce a very large amount of energy. In fact, if we could completely convert the very small mass of a paper clip (0.03 oz) into pure energy using Einstein's formula, we'd have the energy equivalent of 18 kilotons of TNT – roughly the size of bomb that destroyed Hiroshima!

Now let's look at the leadership version of $E=mc^2$:

E represents your organization's **energy**

m represents **mass** – the people within your organization

c^2 represents **your leadership energy** and **the multiplier effect it has on your organization**

Recall in Einstein's theory how c^2 is the secret to unlocking energy from mass? It's no different in this equation, in which c^2 represents the power of your leadership. Your organization already contains an awesome amount of energy, but only the force of your leadership can release it and multiply it in your organization. In fact, the mathematical notation c^2 aptly illustrates the *exponential effect* that a leader can have on multiplying the energy that exists within an organization.

The Conductors of Leadership Energy

After the leader has released the awesome energy of an organization, is the leader's task complete?

No, the leader then must take a very important second step: to conduct that energy and focus it appropriately throughout the organization.

You're probably already familiar with the concept of an energy conductor – a medium that transmits energy, either along it or through it. To use an everyday example, your cookware is an energy conductor that allows you to focus heat energy to accomplish your goal: cooking dinner.

Leadership energy must be conducted, too, so that it can be focused to accomplish the organization's goals. There are five key energy conductors available to us as leaders:

+ Synchronization – the leader can ensure that all the parts of the organization are synchronized and working together toward a common goal.

+ Speed – the leader can resolve conflicts quickly and bring swift, decisive action if adjustments are required in the organization's strategic focus or management procedures.

+ Communication – the leader can connect the team members to corporate goals and ensure everyone understands their role in accomplishing the mission.

+ Customer Focus – the leader can focus the organization on connecting with its customers and creating customer loyalty, which in turn will provide the profits necessary for continued growth.

+ Integrity – the leader can ensure the organization adheres to fundamental values like honesty and truth in everything it does. However, unlike the other conductors, integrity is more like a master switch for the organization. If integrity is compromised, the other conductors are unnecessary since the organization's energy will be entirely depleted and the organization itself may be irreparably harmed.

Let's use an example to demonstrate how all these concepts work together in an organization.

A team leader leaves an organization, but the team members continue to bring energy to all their tasks. After a while, though, and despite their best efforts, the team members find that without a leader their work lacks direction and purpose, and one by one they lose their energy and vitality. Before you know it, productivity lags, quotas are missed, and the once-energetic team members lose their effectiveness.

Now, assume instead that after a short period this team gains a new leader who is committed to the goals and ideals of the organization. Before long, the efforts of the team gain momentum and direction. As the leader grows in her role, she ensures the team is synchronized and working toward the same goals, she encourages communication throughout her organization, and she models integrity in all her relationships. In response, the team members are continually re-energized, and they achieve even more. This leader has very effectively released the energy of her team, conducted it through the right channels, and focused it on achieving goals. Together, this team will have a powerful impact!

Positive vs. Negative Energy

Organizational energy can be either positive or negative. Positive energy, which promotes passion, satisfaction and other affirmative emotions among team members, is possible when the team is focused on shared activities that support the organization's goals.

Negative energy, on the other hand, results in tension and fear among team members, who often feel threatened. But if there is a high level of negative energy, it does not necessarily have to be a destructive force. In fact, this negative type of atmosphere is sometimes a good short-term motivator for intensely competitive team members who thrive on a seek-and-destroy mentality and can unite with other members against a common "enemy." But for long-term, sustained success, extreme negative energy will divide team members and work against the organization.

Actually, a far greater threat to an organization, and a much more common problem, is an energy leak. We'll explore that in the next chapter.

THE FORMULA SUMMARY

$$E = mc^2$$

E is Energy

M is Your People

c^2 is the Leader's Impact

Leadership Energy Conductors:

✦ Synchronization

✦ Speed

✦ Communication

✦ Customer Focus

✦ Integrity

CHAPTER TWO

WHY ENERGY LEAKS OCCUR

The only source of knowledge is experience.

– Albert Einstein

Remember your first helium-filled balloon? Remember the special feeling of walking along with the balloon tied to your wrist, letting it float above your head? When you took it home you let it float to the ceiling of your bedroom. No matter how many times you pulled it down that first day, the balloon was so filled with helium it always floated back up to the ceiling.

But the next morning, you awoke to find a sad blob of latex on the floor. What had happened to that cool balloon that was floating on the ceiling when you went to bed? From the outside, nothing appeared to have changed – there were no holes, and the ribbon was still tied tightly around the end. But even so, the helium had leaked out, and the once-mighty balloon had lost its ability to stay aloft.

The same thing happens to some organizations. For a while the organization is so filled with energy that it seems to soar, and the sky's the limit. But then, slowly and irreversibly, the energy eventually leaks out, and the organization becomes a mere shadow of its former self. Perhaps from the outside nothing obvious has happened, but somehow, the energy that sustained it has disappeared, sometimes seemingly overnight. What was once a super-energized group now struggles to achieve the organization's goals.

How does it happen? Most likely it's because the energy is leaking. If so, quick action will be needed to stop the leak and replenish or replace the energy.

Energy leaks within an organization happen for three key reasons: burnout, comfort in the status quo, or decay.

The Burnout Energy Leak

If an organization is constantly pushed beyond its limits by leaders trying to drive it to spectacular short-term results, it will eventually burn out and begin leaking energy. If every month is a "crisis," soon the organizational norm is in the crisis mode. Not many people can function effectively in the crisis mode all of the time. They will eventually burn out.

Organizational crisis leading to burnout can be caused by a super-charged market or by sudden or drastic downsizing, which can stretch employees too thin. It may occur because of an overzealous production schedule, overtime hours, lost weekends, or lack of a break between new product rollouts.

Do you remember the heady days of the 1990s when the dot.com boom was followed by the dot.com bust? As the dot.com bubble kept growing, leaders earned enormous bonuses, software developers gained VIP status, and sales records soared into the stratosphere – and what could be better? Unfortunately for some organizations, energy began seeping out because continued overexertion made it difficult to think about anything other than maintaining the drumbeat that gradually became louder and louder, faster and faster. The energy was being burned out of organizations of all sizes. For many, the focus was on the "right now" with little time and energy devoted to the long-term results. There were few strategies being implemented that would help them sustain energy and keep energy in reserve to survive not only tomorrow, but also the next day and the next day after that.

Fortunately, many organizations did have energy in reserve after the dot.com bust, and as a result were agile enough to move into the next generation of business. Others, however, especially those unaware of their energy leaks, were unable to adjust and finally collapsed.

To stop the burnout leakage of energy, it's important to understand that organizations function best when there's a rhythm – intense energy surges followed by less intense phases. No organization can maintain the highest level of intensity for an extended period of time. That would be like driving your car at maximum speed all of the time. Eventually, you'd blow out your engine. Your organization, just like your automobile, requires consistent maintenance, re-fueling and tune-ups.

The Status Quo Energy Leak

After a long period of success in a fairly stable environment, sometimes the energy of an organization leaks out because the organization grows too comfortable with the status quo. People become lulled into doing things the way they've always done them, and resist making the changes that are needed to restore energy and improve performance.

Or, sometimes status quo energy leaks occur after a long period of lackluster performance, during which the organization has lost confidence. In either case, the result is that the organization is weak and lifeless, and often it becomes unable to recharge and leverage its resources.

With a status quo energy leak, employees have a relatively high satisfaction level without having high emotions. In fact, low-intensity emotions are usually the hallmark of companies satisfied with the status quo.

Because everyone is satisfied – in their jobs and by their performance – these companies are marked by weak vitality, low levels of alertness, and insufficient stamina to make changes. If the words, "But we've always been successful doing it this way" are familiar, it's time to check your organization's energy level to ensure you're not being lulled into inertia by the status quo.

To prevent the status quo energy leak, you must have a feedback system in place with your team, your customers, and other external sources. If asked for their opinion, they will provide you with the information you need to progressively move forward. Internal feedback alone has the potential to contribute to the status quo energy leak.

There is nothing that is a more certain sign of insanity than to do the same thing over and over and expect the results to be different.

– Albert Einstein

The Decay Energy Leak

The third type of energy leak happens because of decay in an organization, which may be the worst and most toxic leak of all. This type of leak typically occurs when the organization is struggling with both external and internal problems. Typically, the energy that the organization once used to compete is divided and compartmentalized to address both internal and external problems.

General Motors is an example of an organization that's been hit hard by a combination of internal and external issues. Battered by a quadruple whammy – stiff foreign competition, the financial problems of its GMAC Finance subsidiary, falling demand for fuel-hungry SUVs, and labor issues with the United Auto Workers union – it's no surprise that GM lost its energy. In the first quarter of 2007, GM suffered a record loss and huge layoffs.

Many times, energy leaks are solely the result of internal issues. The small, seemingly insignificant internal leaks are subtle and, over time, will drain energy from an organization. Some of the most common are:

+ time and energy spent in unproductive and ineffective meetings

+ lack of clarity in communication resulting in inefficient processes and procedures

+ paralyzing forward movement because of the fear of making difficult decisions

+ power struggles while jockeying for power and position

+ lack of a positive organizational culture and nourishing a victim-mentality culture by allowing blaming and complaining

The energy lost through these seemingly small leaks could easily make the difference between surviving and prospering.

The Road to Energy Recovery

Once energy begins leaking, is survival possible? Let's take a look at Motorola for inspiration.

Once the king of information technology, Motorola came to be known as The Bleeding Giant. Its vibrant energy all but gone, the company found itself at the back of the pack after aggressive competitors raced ahead with new technology. Although it was slow off the mark in reacting, Motorola immediately began turning around with new leadership and new strategies .

The new leadership team utilized energy conductors to stop the bleeding. They created energy by moving forward with renewed vision, passion and hope. They formulated a plan to make sure that everything they did was in alignment with their corporate objectives. They developed a communication process to ensure that everyone knew how they fit into the goals of recovery. They made quick decisions to help them move forward.

Motorola listened to their customers. They recaptured their customer's trust with an innovative lineup of new products, including the red-hot RAZR™ line. They opened up new markets and began shopping their products in European and Asian markets − proof positive it could still design extremely creative products in a saturated industry.

This doesn't mean that revitalizing corporate energy is easy. Far from it. The task of replenishing an organization's energy is not for the faint of heart. It requires a dedicated leadership team to understand why the leaks occurred and to develop a plan to revitalize the energy within the organization.

Energy Leaks Summary

If energy is leaking from your organization, the first step must be to identify the cause. If you determine it's a huge leak, perhaps it was caused by a sudden or dramatic event – burnout, the comfort of the status quo, or decay – or perhaps the loss has resulted from the cumulative effect of smaller energy leaks over time.

Second, learn from the energy loss and regroup. In most cases, the best choices for re-creating organizational energy start from within with an inspiring new vision, a simplified mission, or new organizational values. We'll take a quick look at some of those in the next chapter.

ENERGY LEAKS

+ Burnout – Constant, intense energy over an extended period of time

+ Status Quo – Long periods of consistent performance without new challenges

+ Decay – Leaks that result from failure to address external or internal issues

CHAPTER THREE

MASS – BUILDING THE RIGHT ORGANIZATION

Measured objectively, what a man can wrest from
truth by passionate striving is utterly infinitesimal.

– Albert Einstein

Merriam-Webster Unabridged Dictionary defines *mass* as "an aggregate of particles or things making one body." And that is precisely how we will define the mass in our Leadership Energy equation. In business, mass is the aggregate of employees that make up the organization. Therefore, every organization has mass, and this mass is critical to the organization's growth and continuance.

The people on your team – the mass – possess tremendous potential to achieve your goals and ensure your success. However, you must first ensure you have an organization capable of producing energy by putting the right people in the right places.

Identifying Energizers and Sappers

In theory, every person on your team is a source of energy for your organization. But in reality, some team members create energy while others sap or destroy energy. If you know your team well, you already know which team members are sappers and who are the energizers.

A team full of energized people is easy to manage – their energy just requires focus. It's fun to watch a group of high-energy performers test the limits and spur each other on to even greater results.

At the other end of the spectrum are the sappers. You know who they are – they complain and whine, and think of every reason possible why plans and strategies will not work. They blame others for their issues and don't accept responsibility for what they control. Their negativity and cynicism effectively saps the energy right out of the room.

Your organizational energy is not the sum of your individuals. It is dependent upon the ratio of energizers to sappers. If you have more sappers than energizers, the energy will be drained, and in fact the energizers may eventually become sappers. As unfortunate as it is, a negative, cynical person has a far greater impact on the energy of the team than a positive person.

Many people think having a sapper on the team is better than having no team member at all. If the sapper works in isolation, that may be true. However, since most employees are part of a team or a department, a sapper is usually worse than not having anyone at all. The reason: One sapper on a team of energizers is like one dead battery with three energized batteries in the remote control. Eventually the dead battery, or the sapper, will drain the energy from the others. As a leader you must prevent the sappers from destroying the energizers.

Critical Mass

"Critical mass" is a term with both scientific and social foundations. In the scientific realm, it means the number or amount large enough to produce a specific action or desired result. It takes a certain amount of material – the critical mass – to initiate a nuclear reaction. Less material…no reaction.

In social terms, critical mass represents the point at which there exists enough momentum in a movement for the movement to sustain itself and even expand on its own. As an example: "The national uproar over drug abuse has reached critical mass in Washington."

In business, we can define critical mass as the point at which enough employees act in such a way to cause a shift in the entire organization. It is also the point at which the desired shift becomes a movement capable of sustaining and growing itself. Culture change is a prime example. You won't see a shift in the organization's culture until enough individuals change their attitude, thinking and behavior.

With respect to organizational energy, the goal is to achieve critical mass – the point at which enough individuals are maximizing their energy that the energy of the entire organization is increased.

How many employees does it take to achieve critical mass? Two? Twenty? Two hundred? Two thousand? The answer depends on many factors – the size of the organization, the current culture, leadership's effectiveness and the level of trust that exists between leadership and employees, just to name a few. And let's face it – you're never going to get *every* employee to do anything.

If you want to create change in an organization, you have to get to critical mass. You will achieve critical mass when momentum overtakes inertia. You will achieve an increase in organizational energy, for instance, when the forward momentum of the energizers in your organization exceeds the negative effects (or the inertia) of the energy sappers.

How do you achieve critical mass? It can be created by a large, sweeping factor such as a sudden shift in market conditions or the development of a revolutionary product. These tend to galvanize enough employees to create a permanent change. However, in most organizations, critical mass can be reached through:

1. Establishing dedication to the organization's mission

2. Building a commitment to shared values

3. Creating *leadership* critical mass

Dedication to the Mission

The first critical step in aligning the organization is ensuring that everyone is on board with the organization's mission. Ideally that means every employee should buy into the leadership's vision of where the organization is headed. Buy-in happens when your team understands, commits and takes action to support your organization's goals.

A large oil exploration company that wanted to improve its safety record tried several approaches, to no avail. Finally, the safety department figured out that its safety program would be successful only if they were able to gain the buy-in of every employee – regardless of title and responsibilities.

As with most new initiatives, the new safety program really couldn't be just a program. It had to become a way of life throughout the corporation. Management had to convince every employee it was in their best interest to participate.

How'd they do it?

When the new approach to safety was presented, a small group of believers immediately saw the wisdom of trying to do things differently – but in a safer manner. Those people were the catalyst for others to also open their minds to new and different ideas.

Next, the organization's leadership began sharing stories that projected a positive future for the organization – what was in it for the workers if they embraced the new, different, but safer way of doing things.

As one leader explained to his team, "We want to create a culture where all of us go home every night in good shape."

Once all the workers understood the goals of the new safety culture – yes, it was a culture change – and the workers saw how the new culture would impact their future, those employees sitting on the fence slowly but surely joined the early believers. In the next 12 months, the organization's safety record improved almost 50 percent. In addition, both employee satisfaction and customer satisfaction improved, creating more profit for the organization.

Without achieving critical mass (e.g., getting the buy-in of the company's workers at every level), the new safety culture would not have been realized.

People support what they help create. The more you involve your team in any cultural change, the greater your team will become dedicated to the mission.

Commitment to Shared Values

Shared values build trust and link every level of the organization together. They support the identity and mission, providing guiding principles that everyone on your team can aspire to practice. When people work for an organization with values that match their own, they feel a sense of satisfaction, rapport and community.

You'll often find an organization's values posted in its reception area, on its web site, or inside the front cover of its annual report. But values must be more than just a lofty statement that never makes it off the wall or the printed page – they must be at the core of the organization, and each member of the organization must make a concerted effort to uphold them.

Thomas J. Watson, Jr., founder of IBM, understood that you need unyielding corporate values in order to be successful. He said, "I firmly believe that any organization, in order to survive and achieve success, must have a sound set of beliefs on which it premises all its policies and actions. Next, I believe that the most important single factor in corporate success is faithful adherence to those beliefs. And, finally, I believe if an organization is to meet the challenge of a changing world, it must be prepared to change everything about itself – except those beliefs – as it moves through corporate life."

Almost every organization has published values. Even Enron, the most corrupt company in the last century, had published values. Plaques stating their corporate values of Respect, Integrity,

Communication and Excellence covered the walls of Enron. Sounds sort of silly now, doesn't it?

Values written on ink and paper are worthless unless the values become the driving force of the organization.

Leadership Critical Mass

The final critical element to achieving critical mass within the organization's employees is to create *leadership* critical mass. Leaders throughout the organization must be in sync with one another. You can't hope to reach employee critical mass if your leadership team isn't together.

As with employees, the bulk of leadership should be dedicated to the organization's mission and committed to its values. And yet, that alone is not enough to generate leadership critical mass. Leaders throughout the organization should buy into and support all organizational initiatives. The best leaders are also the best followers.

It's not enough for senior leadership to champion a cause, nor is it enough for all front-line supervisors to be on board. Leadership critical mass requires leadership alignment at every vertical level of the organization – from the C-suite to senior leadership to middle managers to front-line supervisors.

Leaders should also be aligned horizontally in the organization. Leadership critical mass involves alignment among leaders in every functional area of the organization rather than just a few departments such as marketing and sales.

Consider the effect on a team if it's evident their leader disagrees with her boss on the latest policy change. Will the members of that team be energized about the change? No, because they see leadership chaos above them. Likewise, if teams in different departments see that their leaders are at odds over a new initiative, will they support the initiative? Not likely. Bottom line: You can't create employee critical mass without first having leadership critical mass.

The Multiplier Effect

Once you have achieved both leadership and employee critical mass, dramatic shifts and redirections of the organization can be created by the smallest of changes, even in the largest companies.

To illustrate how a small change can have a huge impact, let's take a look at the Butterfly Effect – a discovery made by meteorologist Edward Lorenz. Lorenz used computer simulation to track and model weather patterns. He entered data on wind speed, air pressure and temperature into three linked equations. The calculations formed a mathematical loop – the results of the first equation were fed into the second, the results of which were fed into the third equation. The output of the third equation was ultimately the input back into the first equation. By using the mathematical loop calculations, Lorenz found he could predict weather with some accuracy.

Most mathematicians check and re-check their calculations, and Lorenz was no exception. One day while rechecking the results of his complex weather calculations, Lorenz took a shortcut: he entered the same data he'd used previously except he rounded each number to the nearest one thousandth rather than to the nearest one millionth. (For example, 0.506 instead of 0.506127.)

You'd think that this minor adjustment in the data would have only a minor impact on the overall results, perhaps no more than one tenth of one percent, right? Yet when Lorenz examined the results, he was amazed to discover a significant difference in the two calculations. The infinitesimal change he made in the input was magnified by the feedback process in the mathematical loop, and the results were greatly altered. This discovery ultimately led the meteorologist to wonder, "Does the flap of a butterfly's wings in Brazil cause a tornado in Texas?"

Since then, the Butterfly Effect has become a familiar illustration to describe how a small change in a dynamic system can cause a chain of events that leads to large-scale change.

What does this have to do with organizational energy? A lot! When you achieve critical mass – when the effect of your energizers is greater than the effect of your energy sappers – then small changes in leadership can have a significant impact on the organization. This is the multiplier effect of leadership!

Let's suppose your leadership team has communicated a crystal-clear vision of its organizational goals. In addition, every person on the team understands his or her role and is committed to the mission. Without any other leadership activity, the team will perform at a standard, baseline level. But with critical mass, when appropriate leadership energy is applied, the effect will be powerfully amplified.

On the other hand, if there is leadership chaos, those results will also be magnified throughout the organization and create a situation worse than if there were no leadership intervention at all. Leadership chaos drains organizational energy. Leadership focus and direction add energy to the organization.

Each movement within the masses has a multiplier effect. With critical mass, even small leadership changes – positive or negative –

have a tremendous impact. Our job as leaders is to increase the positive energy and move the masses to create the greatest and most positive impact, and to avoid leadership chaos that would have a negative impact.

Measuring Mass and Its Value

Most people will agree that human capital is a key to organizational success. But despite this fact, few organizations develop a comprehensive approach to maximize this resource and release all of the energy of the organization.

Companies generally determine the value of the mass by measuring the number of employees, productivity per full-time equivalent, gross profitability, and the cost of those employees. Without question, all of these indicators are important. But the real value of the mass is found in the energy it can produce. Perhaps we should ask questions such as:

+ How can we increase the energy within our workforce?

+ What are we doing to drain energy from our team?

+ How can we allocate our resources to gain energy?

Although mass has the capacity to generate energy for the organization, it is leadership that either blocks that energy or enables it to flow freely. To truly leverage the value of the mass, leadership must focus organizational energy through the use of the leadership conductors. They are the key to creating and sustaining organizational energy and moving the organization forward. Leadership conductors, therefore, are the focus of Part Two.

Mass Summary

The mass of your organization – its employees – has the potential to make or break your business. As a leader, one of your most important tasks is to build an organization with the right people. You'll then need to identify which team members create positive energy and which drain it so that you can sustain the team's energy level.

Your goal as a leader is to create critical mass within the organization – the point at which enough individuals are maximizing their energy that the energy of the entire organization is increased. To do that, it's crucial that you create a team atmosphere that's aligned with the organization's goals. Energy will be created and sustained only when your team is dedicated to the organization's mission – leadership's vision of where the organization is headed – and committed to the organization's values. You must also achieve leadership critical mass, where leaders at all vertical levels and within all departments of the organization are in sync and aligned.

When you have leadership and employee critical mass, then you can take advantage of the multiplier effect, in which a small positive change in leadership creates a powerful impact throughout the organization. And finally, the value of the mass is not simply the employees themselves, but also their potential to produce organizational energy. Leadership's job is to leverage and release this energy through conductors.

MASS – BUILDING THE RIGHT ORGANIZATION

✦ Team energy is dependent upon the ratio of energizers to sappers.

✦ A shift in organizational culture occurs when you achieve critical mass – when enough individuals change their attitude, thinking and behavior.

✦ The best leaders are also the best followers.

✦ Organizational energy increases when the forward momentum of energizers exceeds the negative effects of the energy sappers.

✦ People support what they help create.

✦ Leadership focus and direction create energy. Leadership chaos drains organizational energy.

Part Two:

The Conductors of Leadership Energy

Synchronization

Speed

Communication

Customer Focus

Integrity

CHAPTER FOUR

THE SYNCHRONIZATION CONDUCTOR

*Any intelligent fool can make things bigger, more complex, and more
violent. It takes a touch of genius – and a lot of courage –
to move in the opposite direction.*

– Albert Einstein

Synchronized swimming, an Olympic sport since 1984, has always fascinated me. The only way to describe it is to call it upside-down ballet. It's beautiful to watch but also very demanding for swimmers, requiring fitness, stamina and flexibility.

Synchronized swimming usually involves a team of swimmers who perform in perfect synchronization to music. The only equipment is a nose clip.

As I've watched synchronized swim competitions, I've wondered how a team can stay perfectly in sync, especially when the team is performing upside-down and under water – neither of which is natural for most human beings. Yet, Olympic-caliber synchronized swim teams work in unison to create a breathtaking performance.

On world-class synchronized swim teams, each member must clearly understand every nuance of the choreography. All members must also know their individual roles, when to perform each move, and how each of them personally contributes to and affects the entire team's performance.

When every swimmer is in sync, the performance can be spectacular. But if even one team member were ever out of sync, chaos would result.

The same thing happens in business. When all elements of your organization are in sync, its performance can be energizing, spectacular and profitable. But when even one aspect of the organization is out of sync, the result can be chaotic – and often unprofitable too!

Synchronized Leadership

Synchronization is absolutely fundamental to your organization. Without synchronization, people lose focus, stagnate and paralyze the organization. Before you know it, forward movement comes to a halt.

Two elements will help you attain synchronization within your organization: simplify your objectives and align your reward system.

1. Simplify Your Objectives

> *Everything should be made as simple as possible, but not simpler.*
> – Albert Einstein

If your people are out of sync with your organization's objectives, perhaps it's because they're confused about what those objectives are. Maybe your objectives are too complex, too illogical or too difficult to comprehend and embrace. People are energized and more productive when they have memorable priorities to pursue.

Or perhaps your people are confused by the dizzying array of organizational objectives. Ever hear of "Corporate Attention Deficit Disorder"? Here's how it happens: One month, management's focus is to increase revenue. The next month, the focus is on decreasing costs. Then the hiring function is the priority, and 30 days later management is focused again on cutting back. Which one do your people choose to be in sync with?

What would happen if the synchronized swim team's choreography was too complicated? Or what would happen if the choreography changed that often? What would result – chaos or synchronization?

If your goals are constantly changing, you can count on constant chaos. Some in your organization will ignore the current goal because experience has taught them that the goal will soon change anyway. Why bother changing course now when another change is probably just around the corner?

You may be thinking that changing direction is not necessarily a bad thing. And of course you're right. Changing direction isn't a bad thing – as long as a crystal-clear mission has been established, and as long as everyone understands that the changes will help them accomplish this mission. If that's true of your organization, change won't lead to chaos. However, I stress again that everything must be in sync *before* the change.

Synchronization can effectively conduct energy *only* if everyone clearly understands what you're trying to accomplish. Simplicity is the key. Every employee should be able to clearly explain the direction the organization is taking and what role they have in achieving success.

O'Reilly Auto Parts is a successful 50-year-old company in the intensely competitive auto parts industry. Some industry insiders say that auto parts is a commodity business with little or no control over customers or success. O'Reilly thinks differently. They believe the future is determined by having every O'Reilly employee in sync with store objectives and with the corporate objectives.

O'Reilly has simplified their objectives by establishing a simple, three-pronged mission. They aim to have the best-trained employees in the industry who deliver service over and above the customer's expectations and who overachieve their productivity targets.

When you walk into an O'Reilly Auto Parts store, you'll immediately feel the impact of that mission. You'll be greeted by a knowledgeable, well-trained associate who understands his mission: take care of the customer. In the home office, upper management clearly understands its mission: support the store personnel and help them achieve the store goals.

O'Reilly's list of priorities has only three words: People, Service, Productivity. Every O'Reilly employee knows the corporate mission and can recite it by heart in well under 30 seconds. If it takes you more time than that to recite your mission, it's probably too complex. Keep it simple.

> *If you can't explain it simply, you do not understand it well enough.*
> – Albert Einstein

2. Align Your Reward System

Sometimes the reward system of the organization is out of sync with the organization's objectives. In fact, your reward system may be rewarding actions that are diametrically opposed to what you want to accomplish.

For example, in some organizations, employees are paid for overtime – which effectively says the slower you produce, the more money you make – but the organization is penalized for missing deadlines. Watch what you're rewarding and make sure it's in sync with your objectives.

In-Sync Jeans

Several years ago, Levi Strauss created an Aspirations Statement of company values to clearly define what the organization wanted to be. Among the values were teamwork, diversity, recognition, integrity, communication and empowerment. Levi's values were certainly not unique, you'll find them on the walls of many organizations.

However, until a few years ago, Levi's employees were rewarded based only on how well they fulfilled their personal job descriptions. Many times, the job descriptions were out of sync with the Aspirations Statement. Understandably confused, employees' job performance suffered.

After a concerted effort, Levi Strauss achieved synchronicity by aligning its business objectives with its corporate aspirations. Every job description, performance review and recognition program was aligned with the corporate aspirations. This leadership adjustment ultimately successfully re-energized the company to record profits.

What Gets Rewarded

A major organization headquartered in the Midwest was growing rapidly based on its ability to fill same-day orders by 5 p.m. every day. A larger facility was in the works but wouldn't be ready for months.

So as growth continued, the orders were being filled later and later, and instead of being shipped at 5 p.m., they were going out the door at 6 or 7 p.m.

Faced with costly service failures and overtime, upper management followed an employee's suggestion and started paying all employees working on the line until 7 p.m., whether or not it took that long to get all the orders out. Employees could go home when all the orders were out the door.

Suddenly, but not surprisingly, the day's shipments were processed and out the door by 5 p.m.

Under the old system, employees were actually being rewarded for staying late by being paid overtime. When the reward system changed so that the reward was the possibility of leaving early, the results changed. The old management axiom of "what gets rewarded gets done" was proven once again!

Creating Energy

Mutual of New York (MONY) is one of the premier U.S. providers of financial protection and wealth management. One of the characteristics that differentiated MONY from its competitors was the high level of energy it was able to maintain. MONY created energy by making a conscious effort to continually provide a challenging array of products for its clients. In addition, its corporate recognition program was geared to reward high levels of production along with high levels of honesty, integrity and work ethic. The emphasis was on communication and sharing knowledge and information. These three aspects of organizational culture at MONY enabled the company to maintain a strong, clear focus on helping people help themselves. Both internally, with its philosophy, and externally, with the products it delivered, the organization's actions were in sync with its stated philosophy.

The MONY sales force was also saturated with repetitive surges of energy by encouraging top performers to assume leadership roles. The top sales performers were selected to become mentors to the new employees and were rewarded with generous financial rewards and recognition. Generation after generation, MONY's top performers fueled the entire company with steady bursts of energy.

By tradition, MONY's philosophy and rewards system empowered employees, particularly the highest fliers, to share their best practices, their skills in generating business and their work ethic with newer staffers. Without question, MONY's success emerged from the clarity of its focus as well as the synchronization of its rewards system, its traditions and its corporate goals.

Synchronization Conductor Summary

Synchronization is fundamental to the efficient functioning of your organization. When all elements of your organization are in sync, you can more efficiently conduct energy throughout the organization for spectacular and profitable results. Without synchronization, however, people lose focus, stagnate and paralyze the organization.

Synchronization can be created in two key ways: First, simplify your objectives so that everyone on the team understands what you're trying to accomplish. And second, align your rewards system with your objectives. When people are not accomplishing your organization's objectives, check out your reward system. You may find your employees are doing exactly what you're paying them to do.

THE SYNCHRONIZATION CONDUCTOR

+ Without synchronization, your organization will be paralyzed, and forward movement will come to a halt.

+ Synchronization can effectively conduct energy only when everyone clearly understands what you're trying to accomplish.

+ Confusion creates corporate attention deficit disorder. Clarity and simplicity lead to synchronization and the accomplishment of objectives.

+ If it takes you more than 30 seconds to recite your corporate mission, it is probably too complex.

+ What gets rewarded gets done.

CHAPTER FIVE

THE SPEED CONDUCTOR

Imagination is everything.
It is the preview of life's coming attractions.

– Albert Einstein

Along Germany's famous high-speed Autobahn freeway system, many accidents are caused by people who are driving too slowly. If you don't keep up with the pace, you get run over. The same theory applies in business, where reacting too slowly will leave you behind the competition. Either you're in the game early or you can't play at all.

The speed conductor applies in many ways, but in its most basic form speed means decisiveness – understanding your goals, priorities, and customers so well that you can make crucial decisions quickly. Speed also means agility and simplicity.

To conduct energy throughout your organization, you may need to react quickly and decisively in three areas: in organizational strategies, in your management approach, and in conflict resolution.

1. Using Speed to Adjust Strategies

Every successful organization has to be agile and react swiftly to maintain its customers. If your organization can't react to the competitive market quickly enough, your customers will leave you behind.

Wal-Mart is one company that has demonstrated its agility and the ability to change strategies rapidly. It's become the largest retail company in the world through its ability to quickly capitalize on the newest technology to manage inventory, distribute products and handle cash. Wal-Mart uses technology to track customer buying trends and make quick decisions about which inventory needs to be available in each store. Sam Walton learned early on that speed could be the primary differentiator that would allow his organization to deliver the lowest prices to their customers.

In its early days, Dell Computer built its reputation by focusing on speed and simplicity. Instead of distributing computers through the usual retail outlets, Dell directly connected its manufacturing line to the customer, simplifying the purchase process and eliminating several steps in between. Its bold strategy back then was to build a computer to the customer's specifications and send it directly to the customer, quickly setting itself apart with its speed, personalized products and quality. Dell realized a simple business model – dealing directly with the consumer – was a better approach than the complexity of adding additional channels. Although its distribution and sales channel strategy has changed and now they have multiple streams of distribution, Dell originally created a new market niche by focusing on speed.

Re-Strategize Me

A few years ago, filmmaker Morgan Spurlock produced a documentary called *Super Size Me*, which skewered the fast-food industry by chronicling his month-long experiment.

To test the health effects of a fast-food diet, for one month Spurlock ate three meals a day at McDonald's. The results were frightening: his weight shot up more than a pound a day, and his triglycerides and cholesterol went through the roof. Twenty days into filming his doctors begged him to stop.

The movie's release, just months after two teenage girls had sued McDonald's for causing their obesity (and lost) dealt a blow to the McDonald's brand.

To regain its energy in the marketplace and make up for lost market share, McDonald's made several significant, agile moves to adjust its corporate strategies: the company icon, Ronald McDonald, abandoned his clown costume and donned exercise clothing; heart-healthy items like salads and fresh fruit were added to the menu; CDs and exercise DVDs were offered with certain menu items; and nutritional information was printed on food wrappers.

Perhaps the most significant move was the hiring of Mary Dillon, former president of Quaker Foods, as executive vice president, global chief marketing officer and leader of McDonald's "Balanced Lifestyle Initiatives."

What would have happened if McDonald's just sat back and waited for the "storm" to pass? Would they have been able to survive all the negative publicity? We do not know, but we do know that by moving quickly to make strategic adjustments, McDonald's regained its energy and entered into a new era of success.

2. Using Speed in Management Processes

Speed is particularly critical in two key areas of employee relations: recognizing employees who perform, and dealing with employees who underperform.

Recognizing Employee Performance

Recognizing positive individual and team performance is an essential ingredient in creating and maintaining organizational energy. Front-line employees stay with an organization for one key reason – because they feel that their supervisors care about them. When employees feel appreciated they perform better, and that translates to less attrition and happier customers.

And it doesn't take much to show you care. Even relatively simple gestures, like writing positive e-mails or promptly returning their calls, go a long way in creating an atmosphere of appreciation. The entire organization is energized by an environment where people are appreciated.

The Beryl and FedEx Way

The Beryl Companies, a leading U.S. customer interaction firm, has been selected as one of the top two Best Medium Size Companies to Work for in America by the Best Place to Work Institute. Why do people enjoy working at Beryl, and why is its turnover rate significantly below the industry average? Beryl does many things extremely well, but the driving force behind employee satisfaction is CEO Paul Spiegelman, who understands the power of positive recognition.

Spiegelman says the emotional environment is where culture is built. And so Beryl laid the foundation with a simple yet powerful personal recognition strategy that's based on sending personal note cards to co-workers every day, recognizing milestones such as anniversaries and birthdays, and helping those in need.

BerylCares is the name of the behind-the-scenes program that gathers information about events in a worker's life. Says Spiegelman, "We can't recognize births, weddings, and other joyful happenings and then turn a blind eye to personal calamities. Instead, we reach out very quickly if someone is going through a rough time due to a health situation, a death in the family or just a patch of rotten luck. If there's anything we can do as a company to help and support them, we want to know about it and acknowledge it. If our culture preaches taking care of our own, the caring has to start in my office."

Acknowledging employees is vitally important to maintaining the organization's energy.

While I was at FedEx, we had a recognition program called Bravo Zulu. In the U.S. Navy, the Bravo Zulu flag means "well done." Every FedEx manager had Bravo Zulu stickers, plaques and Bravo Zulu money they could use to immediately recognize any employee who went above and beyond in an effort to satisfy a customer.

The Bravo Zulu symbol was prominently displayed at every FedEx office. People wore the symbols on their employee badges, put them on their business cards, and posted them at their work stations. Bravo Zulu was a symbol of pride, and it was effective because it was a quick, immediate reward. The Bravo Zulu sticker cost a mere five cents, but the recognition was priceless.

Both Beryl and FedEx understand that acting quickly to recognize employees can have a tremendous impact in building loyalty, respect and trust. Those qualities in turn build positive energy for your organization.

Dealing with Underperformers

As much as you might want to avoid it, it's vital to take quick, decisive action to stop the energy leaks caused by underperformers. These are the people on your team who chronically do as little as they can get away with, or who are simply not right for the job.

Though usually small, this group can have a huge impact because they also prevent the top performers from doing their jobs. To compensate for these underperformers, you're probably loading up your top performers with extra work just so you can meet your deadlines. You don't mean to punish your star performers, but by asking them to take up the slack for non-performers you're punishing them for doing a good job. So what's the incentive for a top performer to keep working at that level? Once they see that mediocrity gets rewarded, they may gravitate to mediocrity, too – exactly the opposite of what you need.

What's worse, the problem of an incompetent employee will not just go away by itself. When people figure out they can do less and still get rewarded, they'll just continue to underperform if there's no reason to do more. And while you're giving them their second or third "one more chance," they could be destroying your team and your organization. The longer an underperformer remains on the team, the more positive energy that will be sapped and the more negative energy that will be created. The leader's job is to reward superstar performance and create new positive energy, so you must deal with the falling stars quickly, decisively and fairly.

You may be saying, "But it takes too long and it's too hard to get rid of the underperformers. It's easier just to move the work around." Yes, it's true that in many organizations it is difficult to fire anybody – and normally speed is not part of the firing process.

But there's a huge price to pay when you allow people to stay around after they've already "quit."

The rules of employee termination are in place to make sure you're fair and consistent – not to prevent you from ridding your organization of someone who's chosen not to work to the performance standards. In fact, your Human Resources department will be a great help if you've done your job by establishing performance standards and providing feedback to your employees about their performance. If you want to fire someone to whom you gave a great performance review just two months ago, don't make the situation worse by blaming HR for making it too tough!

If the employee's performance doesn't improve after you've given feedback to that employee, then even Vince Lombardi wouldn't be able to turn them around. There are reasons for their poor performance, but you don't control those. What you do control is the next move in your organization – do you allow underperformers to stay and drain your team's energy, or should you allow them to move forward with another organization?

Most fired employees will eventually admit that getting fired was the best thing that ever happened. As unbelievable as that may sound, many people who have been fired are forced to move from a job that isn't right for them to something more aligned with their talents and interests. With few exceptions, it's also the best thing for the team and the leader.

Here's an exercise I did several years ago that opened my eyes to the courage it takes to manage varying performance levels:

First, on a flip chart write the name of each team member and then categorize each one as either a superstar or a falling star.

Put their most recent performance review score next to their name, and then pull their personnel file. For each person, note each time that you've documented some kind of recognition or performance improvement over the past six months. It could be a letter of appreciation or a performance improvement document.

You may discover, as I did, that there was little difference between how I treated my top performers and the lowest performers. The issue in my case was not an employee issue – it was a leadership issue of not recognizing and rewarding the behaviors I wanted.

Deal with the underperformer quickly yet fairly. The longer an underperformer remains on the team, the more energy will be sapped from your team!

3. Using Speed to Resolve Conflicts

> *"We can't solve problems by using the same kind of thinking we used when we created them."*
>
> – Albert Einstein

Various studies show that most adversity inside organizations involves interpersonal conflicts within the work group. Those same studies show that very few of these conflicts work themselves out without third-party intervention. So don't make the mistake of ignoring conflicts, hoping they'll just go away. The longer these conflicts are allowed to fester, the more likely they are to drain energy from the work group and from the entire organization.

A popular rule of thumb in dealing with conflicts is called the 1-10-100 rule. You may have heard this rule applied to many situations, but in this context let's call it the "molehills-to-mountains rule." The rule illustrates how a small issue can grow exponentially if left unchecked. The longer it persists, the more difficult and time consuming it is to fix – and the more of your organization's energy it will waste.

You can apply the molehills-to-mountains rule to many situations in an organization – a minor conflict between two team members, a billing discrepancy with a customer, a quality slippage, or a simple misunderstanding with a vendor. According to the 1-10-100 rule, when you contain the conflict and solve it quickly, it is solved with the equivalent of one unit of time, money or resources. If not addressed, however, that same problem can spread into a work group and solving it will require the equivalent of 10 units of time, money or resources. If the problem is allowed to move through the organization or into the customer base, it will then require at least 100 units of measurement to solve – 100 times what it would have cost to solve the same problem in the beginning.

The lesson? Put speed to work in your organization to resolve small conflicts quickly, before they become expensive, company-wide disasters!

"Never leave a nail sticking up where you find it" is an old adage. In other words, don't just ignore minor problems, hoping they'll go away. Address them quickly, as soon as they come up, and you can avoid a much larger problem later.

Speed Conductor Summary

With the pace of change these days, all businesses are in the business of speed. But the speed conductor isn't just about doing things fast. It's about agility and decisiveness.

If your organization has been left behind competitively, or if your strategies are outdated and no longer profitable, show agility and make the necessary changes.

In your management approach, celebrate successes by quickly recognizing high performers. Quick, on-the-spot action to recognize the achievements of employees can have a tremendous impact in building loyalty and respect. And although it's a painful task, take decisive action to clear out the underperformers from your organization. The longer they stay, the more energy they drain.

And finally, if there's a conflict in your organization, don't ignore it. Instead, recognize immediately that it probably won't be resolved without intervention. Act decisively to resolve it before it grows out of control. Large problems consume far too much time, energy and resources that are needed elsewhere in your organization.

THE SPEED CONDUCTOR

+ To remain on top, successful organizations have to be agile and react swiftly to changing conditions.

+ The entire organization is energized by an environment in which people are appreciated.

+ It is vital to take quick, decisive action to stop the energy leaks caused by underperformers.

+ Acting quickly to recognize employees can have a tremendous impact on building loyalty, respect and trust.

+ The longer an underperformer remains on the team, the more energy will be sapped from your team! Address issues quickly to avoid larger problems later.

CHAPTER SIX

THE COMMUNICATION CONDUCTOR

The important thing is not to stop questioning.
Curiosity has its own reason for existing.

– Albert Einstein

There were 20 area vice-presidents seated around the conference table. The rules had been outlined. All VPs knew this was their chance to improve the operation of their organizations. After the facilitator had put everyone at ease, she fired the first question: "What one thing would make the greatest difference in your area?"

One by one, the VPs slid their written responses toward the facilitator. Without exception, every one of them had written "improved communications."

"You can't have too much in the way of communication," said one VP when the results were announced. "It's the foundation of your effectiveness."

According to a communications Return on Investment (ROI) study conducted by Watson Wyatt in 2006, that VP was right. The study found that companies with effective internal communications were 4.5 times more likely than other companies to report high levels of employee engagement. Employee engagement, in turn, had a positive impact on the bottom line:

✦ Companies with the most effective internal communication programs achieved a 91 percent Total Return to Shareholders (TRS) versus a 58 percent TRS among ineffective communicators;

✦ Companies that significantly improved their internal communication effectiveness increased their market share by 19.4 percent.

Communication is an important energy conductor in any organization, continually carrying energy internally to all parts of the organization and externally to customers and vendors.

But how do you create this communications conductor? Build numerous small meeting rooms throughout corporate headquarters to encourage random conversations? Start a company newsletter? Make sure every employee gets a copy of the annual report? No. The most important element of the communications conductor is to connect the corporate goals and objectives with the activities of your team.

Some elements of effective communications can include:

✦ using technology to connect employees

✦ creating a formal communication structure and process

✦ facilitating a connection between employees and customers

+ dealing quickly and directly with issues

+ soliciting employee feedback

+ integrating rewards in the organizational culture

The communication conductor begins even before employees are hired, in the way they're treated in interviews. Communication conductors never end.

Communicating Appreciation to Employees

During a recent exit interview in a large New York City-based corporation, a high-level employee sat across from the organization's president and explained her reasons for leaving. "I've done more than the job required, I've been a loyal employee for almost eight years and I've never had anything but superior performance reviews," she said. "Yet, I have rarely felt appreciated or valued."

The president was dumbfounded. "But we've paid you very well for your efforts," he responded after a moment.

"But I need more than the money," the employee answered.

"Our benefits are some of the best in the industry."

"But I need more than benefits," the woman said. "I need to know that I'm worth the same care and concern I give every one of my customers – and to be honest, I've never sensed that from this organization." Even though the employee was well paid, good at her job, and valued by corporate, she felt that the organization really didn't care about her. The organization's emphasis on pay and benefits was not as important to her as the very simple act of making sure she knew that someone cared about her.

In 1998, study results published in the *Harvard Business Review* noted that retailing giant Sears reported a 4 percent increase in employee satisfaction. This increase, in turn, resulted in an identical increase in customer satisfaction and a rise of more than $200 million in revenue. Coincidence? Not likely.

Southwest Airlines' mission statement says: "Above all, employees will be provided the same concern, respect and caring attitude within the organization that they are expected to share externally with every Southwest customer." At Southwest, management expects employees to "give as good as they get" – and the yield is very high. Employees treat customers with care and compassion because that's what the organization provides for them – and this corporate culture keeps customers coming back, year after year.

To conduct energy through your organization, you must stay connected through good communication.

"As one example, at Southwest, leaders and managers are taught in training classes to write commendation letters for their employees," explained Lorraine Grubbs-West, author of *Lessons in Loyalty: How Southwest Airlines Does It – An Insider's View.* "Employees are encouraged to commend their fellow workers – and Southwest tries to make it easier by providing simple forms called stroke sheets."

Every time a stroke sheet is written, two things happen: First, the person who wrote the letter receives a letter of thanks from the company for commending a fellow employee. Second, the employee being recognized receives a copy of the commendation plus a thank you from the department head.

"At Southwest, we identified 'internal customers' as well as 'external customers,'" Grubbs-West explained. "The pilots' major internal customers, for example, were the mechanics. Obviously planes couldn't fly unless they were serviced. For flight attendants, their 'internal customer' was the Provisioning Department. The attendants couldn't do their jobs if the provisions weren't there.

"To show their appreciation of these internal customers, groups would 'adopt' each other. Every quarter, they would do something to show their appreciation. Pilots regularly showed up at 2 a.m. and flipped burgers or cooked barbecue dinners for the mechanics who worked from 11 p.m. to 7 a.m."

According to *Inventive Incentives*, a manual the airline published for its management, it costs very little to let employees know how much they're appreciated and how valuable they are. "It can be as simple as decorating an employee's cubicle in honor of one of their life's special events," Grubbs-West remembered, "or perfect attendance lunches or a birthday cake to celebrate someone's birthday."

Grubbs-West, who taught leadership classes during her tenure at Southwest, introduced her classes to the airline's unique culture when she encouraged managers to get to know their people, one of the distinctions that continue to contribute to Southwest's unprecedented success. Southwest treats their team members as people who have real needs – not as just an employee number. In return, their employees reward them with loyalty – Southwest's turnover rate is the best in the industry.

"When I taught leadership at the University for People, we introduced an 'ancient Japanese leadership style' called GTHOOYO, demonstrating a karate chop as we chanted 'Getoyo!'" recalled Grubbs-West.

"Actually, this leadership style didn't originate in ancient Japan, but was the acronym for 'Get the Heck out of Your Office!' – also known as Management by Walking Around and an extremely important part of Southwest's leadership philosophy."

These communications conductors – spoken, written and demonstrated – have continued to energize Southwest Airlines and have helped propel it to its position as the nation's most consistently profitable airline.

Good Communication Begins Internally

Unfortunately, very few organizations are completely satisfied with their internal communications. No matter how many workshops are conducted, how much emphasis it's given and how many e-mails or memos are circulated, organizations rarely have the clear communication channel that they envisioned.

However, that's no excuse to stop making an effort! It's important to *continue* making every effort to enhance your internal communications at every level of your organization.

The strength of your internal communications parallels how well you connect and communicate with your external audiences – customers, vendors and the community. If employees are able to work seamlessly across departmental functions to provide an extraordinary customer experience, results will improve – guaranteed.

At one major corporation, leadership realized there were problems with internal communications. Departments weren't communicating well. Managers weren't all hearing the same messages during staff meetings. Yet the CEO didn't give it much thought. "People make mistakes," he reasoned. "Nobody's perfect." However, as one client after another moved their business to a competitor, the CEO began focusing his undivided attention on the bottom line. "Why are we losing customers?"

The list of reasons wasn't pretty.

Deliveries were late. Service was haphazard. Dispatching was sloppy. Product reliability was suffering. In fact, during a focus group session, former clients indicated that every problem they'd experienced could be traced back to communication issues.

At the end of the meeting, the focus group facilitator summed up the results: "Your people aren't communicating well, internally or externally. Your organization appears in disarray to your clients. Processes seem chaotic. You're going to have to repair your image, for starters, and while you're doing that, you need to work on both sides of your communication – internal and external."

After much thought, the CEO began to consider the facilitator's suggestions. His first inclination was to tweak the system already in place, but then he thought better of it. Perhaps it would take more than tweaking. He called in an informal communication task force of managers, team leaders and employees. After some discussion, he thought the task force had come up with a better strategy.

After reflecting on the communication process within his organization, the CEO determined that:

+ **It matters what they hear, not what you say.** A two-way process is essential to the communication conductor. Every employee may have a different interpretation of what you say. Without a feedback mechanism, the conductor will not work.

✦ **It matters what they read, not what you write.** E-mail and text messaging are great communication tools for some things. However, no one can read your mind. Be crystal clear in all your communication and leave as little as possible open to interpretation.

✦ **If there's no trust of leadership, none of what you say or do matters anyway.**

Good Communication Means Good Listening

In 1837, Hans Christian Andersen wrote *The Emperor's New Clothes*, a classic fable. As with all fairy tales, though, the story about the vain and powerful Emperor has important lessons to teach us. Believe it or not, I think this fable has several terrific leadership lessons.

You're probably familiar with Andersen's tale, but just in case you're not, I'll remind you that the gist is that the Emperor goes naked in a parade because everyone is afraid to tell him the truth about his new suit. It takes a small child to point out the obvious, but by then it's much too late to fix this embarrassing situation.

The moral of the story for leaders is that we shouldn't get so caught up in our own leadership positions that we're afraid to ask for feedback. Good communication is a two-way street, and you need to listen just as much as you speak.

But more important, you must first create an atmosphere where honest feedback and suggestions are welcomed, without recourse. Does your team feel comfortable telling you the truth, or do they feel they have to tell you what you want to hear? If your team is intimidated by the power of your position or the pressure to conform to the majority, sooner or later you could also be like the Emperor and get caught in an embarrassing position.

Asking for feedback, and really listening to what is said, is an effective way to energize your organization. If you're willing to listen, the people in your organizations will usually be willing to tell you what you need to know.

Communicating Above Distractions

You'd think that with all of our electronic communication devices, we'd be better at actually communicating. But too often, those technological marvels become nothing more than distractions. Remember when we used to complain about the telephone always ringing? I miss those simpler times! Now we have to deal with voice mail, e-mail, cell phones, PDAs, Podcasts, 24-hour news channels and text messaging – and sometimes even the telephone!

More times than we realize, these distractions cloud the message of our communications, so what we *say* and what they *hear* are two entirely different things. Remember, some people process audio information best, while others who are more visual prefer written messages. Some people process just the words of a message while others look for messages in body language, facial expressions, posture, clothing styles and other subtle cues. With all of these extra considerations, it's no wonder that our messages sometimes get skewed or even obscured entirely.

Whether we like it or not, the person receiving our communication decides whether our communication is successful. Effective, connected communication is not about you – it's about them. It's not about the message that gets *transmitted* – it's about the message that gets *received*. But you can help this communication process enormously by transmitting each message accurately, consistently, simply and effectively.

For instance, if you've ever had telephone training, someone probably encouraged you to smile when you talk on the phone. It really works – it's possible to "hear" the smile in your voice. That's a very simple beginning to successful communication.

The same care and awareness should go into every written communication. Is the message well worded? Is it free of spelling and grammatical errors? Is it spare and efficient, or did you use 15 words when you only needed 10? Does the message convey what you want to say? Is it clear and concise?

And finally, don't let technology distract you from your message. You need to communicate above the distractions, so choose the best communications method for the message you need to get out. If you're e-mailing or texting a message, are you providing enough information to clearly communicate? Or is the message so short that it's confusing? Will you need to send a follow-up e-mail or two, or even schedule an audio conference call to clear up the confusion?

Communicating Knowledge

One of the best investments of your time is to teach your team the business of your business. People have a basic need to understand how they fit into a worthwhile cause.

Learning creates energy. You can create a strategic advantage for your organization by providing resources for your team members to learn and share knowledge. Knowledge shared is energy multiplied because it's contagious.

IBM learned long ago that an educated workforce creates energy, so the company's training goes far beyond the training department. They have unleashed knowledge by giving their employees the resources to learn on their own. The IBM philosophy is to provide every employee the opportunity to create a thirst for continuous growth.

Teach the business of your business

Ritz-Carlton is one of the best-known and finest hotel chains in the world. Customer service is more than just a slogan for this company – it's a unique way of doing business.

Ritz-Carlton is consistently among the highest-rated hotels in the world, and that's because of how its staff communicates knowledge. Before every shift, teams meet for 10 minutes to share critical information, and each employee receives a small packet with the day's vital information. These brief meetings eliminate confusion and ensure that everyone knows the day's priorities.

Sharing knowledge and teaching employees the business of the business helps build understanding. The more information leaders share about the "why" behind the "what" they are trying to accomplish, the more energized the organization becomes.

Another highly successful hotel leader, Bill Marriott, believes the seven most important words a leader can say are: "I don't know...what do you think?"

Most of the time, the people on the team already know how to solve any organizational problem – you just need to ask them. When you listen with the intent to act on their suggestions, you create energy.

The 95/5 Rule

Most organizations inadvertently operate under the "95/5" rule, meaning that workgroups understand about 95 percent of what goes on inside their own departments, but only 5 percent of what goes on in other parts of the organization.

Only 5 percent? Doesn't it seem they should know more about other parts of the organization? Wouldn't things work better if the team could see the big picture? You'll create energy in your organization if you "tear down the walls" between departments and show teams how each discipline contributes to the organization.

One organization "tears down the walls" by periodically holding an Employee Awareness Week, during which every department conducts a workshop to communicate what they do and how it fits into the big picture. At the end of the week, the whole company is energized because everyone understands how other teams contribute to the organization's success.

Shared knowledge creates positive energy!

Energy Multiplied

In July 2006, Comcast introduced a radical training process for customer-service agents called Comcast Bullseye, an on-demand, targeted learning program to train customer-service reps both professionally and personally. The program has been instrumental in helping to meet the company's business objectives through performance and process improvement.

What makes Bullseye unique is that it's available on demand, meaning there are no formal beginning or ending dates. The program has three stages:

First, new customer-service reps complete a baseline assessment of their knowledge.

Then the Comcast facilitators, who take on the role of performance coaches, use these assessments to tailor a training program and to know where to direct each new employee for more training. Depending on what they need to know, employees are directed to online learning, web sites, performance-support systems or internal knowledge bases.

The performance coaches are a vital part of the training. They direct employees to various resources but they're no longer the only source of information. The coach's job is to build a community of knowledge that can be shared throughout the organization. Learners also complete hands-on lab work, working with the company billing system and role-playing with peers.

The third phase of the training, BITS – Bringing It Together – is an integration phase where the new employees integrate all of their learning into a complex working environment. New employees role-play customer interactions and demonstrate all the skills they've learned.

Comcast has found a way to multiply energy and to share knowledge throughout their organization. The result is that the customer-service agents understand much more than customer service. They understand the business of Comcast and the effect they have on Comcast's success.

Energizing Mondays

I believe that Monday is the most important day for organizational energy. Every Monday, the tone is set for the week. If Mondays are dreaded, the energy of the organization is sapped. If Mondays are greeted with anticipation, the organization is energized. Monday is the key to your work week!

Most organizations don't have to worry about energizing Fridays – that comes naturally! In fact, for most people, the most energized day is the day before they go on vacation. They get things done – fast!

What if your Mondays created 10 percent more energy for your organization? What if your Mondays were just as productive as the last day before your vacation? That could make the difference between just surviving or prospering.

All you have to do is make Monday your day for organization-wide learning and development. Below is the game plan outlined in *Monday Morning Choices* to create organizational energy by Changing Your Mondays and Changing Your Life:

1. Find at least five people at your office who will join you on your *Change Your Monday – Change Your Life* journey. Find people who want to move forward and are willing to pay a small price to improve their lives. Only about one hour a week is required – 40 minutes of prep work plus a 20-minute meeting every Monday morning.

2. Make sure everyone has a *Monday Morning Choices* book. During the week, every person should read the chapter that will be discussed the following Monday. An even more effective approach is to read and discuss the chapter at home with a partner before you talk about it with your team at work.

3. Arrive at work 20 minutes early for the next 12 Mondays, prepared to discuss the choices revealed in the chapter of the week.

4. Make a commitment to do something different, based on the chapter your group is discussing.

5. Begin changing your Mondays and changing your life!

Once you have taken your staff through *Monday Morning Choices*, choose another book and keep the energy flowing. This process facilitates learning and the sharing of knowledge throughout the organization. Don't be surprised to discover that the more people learn, the more energized they become at work.

The Communication Conductor Summary

Good communication can be a powerful way to energize your organization from the top down and to connect your employees to your customers.

But good communication doesn't just happen – it takes a willingness to always seek improvements to the communication process. To improve communication within your organization, let employees know they're appreciated, tell them you want their feedback, and then actually listen to their feedback. Communication is a two-way process. Make sure you communicate above the distractions – technological and otherwise – to ensure the message you're sending to your team is the message they're receiving.

Finally, continue creating energy by communicating knowledge about the business and by promoting a culture of learning.

THE COMMUNICATION CONDUCTOR

✦ If there is no trust, it doesn't matter what you communicate.

✦ Don't get so caught up in your leadership position that you're afraid to ask for honest, candid feedback.

✦ Effective communication is not about you – it's about them!

✦ Knowledge shared is energy multiplied.

✦ Bill Marriott's seven most important leadership words: "I don't know…what do you think?"

✦ The more people learn, the more energized they become at work.

CHAPTER SEVEN

THE CUSTOMER FOCUS CONDUCTOR

Sometimes one pays the most for the things one gets for nothing.

– Albert Einstein

How would you like to sell a product that's already sold on almost every street corner? This product has been around for a thousand years, give or take, but you're supposed to come up with a new angle on it, all while ignoring recent medical advice about the possible health hazards of consuming this product. And what's more, you're required to sell this well-known and readily available commodity for four or five times more than your competitors do. Sound like a lousy business plan?

One of the most successful companies in the world, Starbucks, does exactly that.

Starbucks coffee is not significantly different than the coffee you can buy at any convenience store. Their cups are not any better or nicer. And to top it off, while the convenience store sells coffee for around $1, Starbucks sells essentially the same thing for more than $4, quite a jump in price. Yet customers willingly line up to buy coffee and other drinks from Starbucks.

So, what is Starbucks doing better than anyone else?

The reason people choose to pay more for Starbucks coffee is because of the connection this company has made with its customers. It provides a customer-friendly atmosphere where people are comfortable just hanging around, answering e-mails or studying – and the longer they hang around, the more they buy. By creating this connection, Starbucks has transformed a commodity purchase into an experience that's a necessary part of the day for millions of customers around the world.

Making connections with your customers will energize your entire organization, and it will also allow you to meet and exceed customer expectations.

Most customers aren't unreasonable – but they do have needs. They need to be listened to, paid attention to and treated with respect. And if you can eliminate hassle and stress from their decisions, customers will become loyal to your organization.

The Impact of the Customer Focus Conductor

Focusing on the customer creates long-term customer loyalty, which will energize your entire organization and ensure lasting organizational success. Can you name any organization that gets positive referrals from *un*happy customers? In fact, even just a few unhappy customers can tremendously affect your bottom line because they tend to be very loud, very opinionated and very public in their dissatisfaction.

The Power of the Customer Focus Conductor

Every organization wants new customers. New customers create energy, and that is great. However, the energy new customers create cannot begin to compensate for the energy that is lost when unhappy customers move on to a competitor. Even if you're gaining five customers a week, if you're losing another five, you're on a downward spiral.

Why? Because an unhappy customer who defects will tell an average of 16 people why he was dissatisfied with your service. The new customer might tell an average of two people why he is satisfied – if you're lucky.

That's why it's so crucial to focus on your customers, identify their needs, connect with them and keep them happy. Customer focus is vital in generating day-to-day energy and in sustaining energy as your business grows.

Loyal customers create more powerful energy than new customers. Loyal customers are proof that whatever you're doing, you're doing it right! Let's look at how focusing on retaining loyal customers can make a difference over time.

Let's imagine two customer-focused companies, A and B, which compete in the same industry. Each has 100 customers and each is adding new customers at a rate of 15 percent per year. By working extra hard to keep its customers happy, Company A retains 95 percent of its customers each year, while Company B retains 90 percent. That 5 percent doesn't sound like a big difference, does it? However, that small difference will compound over time to result in a large difference. You can see the impact of customer retention below:

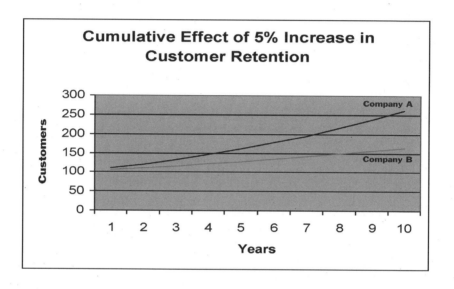

Even though both companies are adding 15 percent more customers each year, because Company A has retained 5 percent more customers each year, after 10 years Company A has 60 percent more customers.

There is no escaping it – the customer focus conductor has a direct impact on your bottom line!

The Customer Focus Conductor Begins With Your Team!

If your customers are unhappy, you'll eventually end up with unhappy employees, too. Constant customer complaints can sap the energy from your organization faster than almost anything. If the customer is always right, and they're always complaining, why would your employees want to stick with you? Who wants to listen to customers complain all day?

But happy customers energize employees. Everybody wants to work for the best!

Let's take another look at Southwest Airlines. If you've ever flown Southwest, you know the flight attendants, gate agents and pilots are some of the nicest, friendliest in the business. When customers are around employees who are proud of their organization energy is increased. The front-line employee becomes an energy conductor.

Nordstrom department store is another high-energy organization that offers legendary customer service. Nordstrom has instilled a "customer first" priority and it shows – the company's employee satisfaction and customer satisfaction ratings are at the top of their industry. Satisfied employees energize customers and satisfied customers energize employees – this conductor runs both ways!

However, in any company, dissatisfied customers and dissatisfied employees become ill-willed ambassadors who affect the organization's reputation. I was reminded of how true that is on a recent weekend trip when we stopped to buy ice cream. When we entered the shop, the employees didn't seem to even notice us. They never smiled and never made eye contact, and after a while, we felt almost apologetic for ordering our ice cream cones. Obviously, those employees were neither happy to be there that day nor proud to work for that employer. We'll probably never stop there again. Without even meaning to, the unhappy employees became ill-willed ambassadors. They sapped the energy from us and ended up creating not only dissatisfied customers but also more ill-willed ambassadors.

Customer Energy Conductor ROI

Here's the most important point: the customer focus conductor has a direct return on investment. Loyal customers are created primarily through outstanding customer connections. People choose to become customers for many different reasons – perhaps because of new product ideas, your ingenious marketing campaigns or your company's reputation. However, in most instances, the real "magic" can be found in how well you have connected with your customer.

It's been shown that customers continue to do business with an organization because of the service they receive. Studies have shown customers defect for reasons that seldom have anything to do with product quality. In fact, most customers leave because they feel the chilly air of indifference – as we did in the ice cream store. The customer who doesn't feel a connection has less reason to return.

Even if you're selling the finest product of its kind, good customers will eventually disappear if a positive connection is missing. Customers need a positive connection.

More than talk…walk the talk!

Every organization talks about focusing on the customer – the slogans blanket the halls of almost every company. These may sound familiar:

- ✦ Customers Are First!

- ✦ We Exist to Serve the Customer!

- ✦ Think Customer!

- ✦ Customer Champions!

- ✦ 100% Customer-Focused!

✦ The Customer is King!

✦ We Are Customer-Driven!

Though the slogans are nice and make great banners and T-shirts, many customers will tell you that in many organizations "customer service" is a contradictory phrase – an oxymoron.

The good news? It doesn't have to be that way!

In fact, improving customer service really comes down to doing a few things extremely well. It begins when the customer focus conductor is in place and working both ways, connecting customer needs with your organization's objectives, and solving the customer's problems with your organization's products and services.

Second-mile service

Chick-fil-A is an incredible success story. Even though the company's stores are only open six days a week – one of their core values is to allow all employees to spend Sunday with family – Chick-fil-A is highly successful in the intensely competitive fast-food industry.

Truitt Cathey, founder of Chick-fil-A, introduced three energizing words to his team: "It's my pleasure."

It's a very simple technique. Whenever you request something, a Chick-fil-A associate always responds, "It's my pleasure." But – and here's the magic ingredient – the energy doesn't come from the voice or the words. It's in the attitude. At Chick-Fil-A, they've created an environment where it truly *is* a pleasure to serve their customers. The organization spends a considerable amount of time attracting employees who really desire to serve the customer.

Chick-fil-A practices what they call "second-mile service." A clean restroom is first-mile service – everyone in the industry can do that. Second-mile service is going beyond what everyone else does and going the extra mile. At Chick-fil-A, it's not unusual to see employees helping someone to the car in the rain, carrying a tray for a mom who has young kids in tow, or picking up wastepaper while conversing with diners. Each of those experiences exhibits second-mile service and allows energy to flow between the customer and employee.

Chick-fil-A is focused on the customer and those who serve the customer. Every Chick-fil-A store bears a plaque engraved with this principle: "Associate yourselves only with those people you can be proud of – whether they work for you or you work for them." Cathey realized early in his business career that if you take care of your people, they will take care of the customers.

The nice customer

How much attention does your organization pay to customer satisfaction? Unfortunately, you can't depend on your customers to provide the feedback you need to conduct energy.

Here's why: There are many types of customers. Some are so nice that you never hear from them, others are always complaining, and still others are somewhere in between. Regardless of how you classify your customers, don't take any of them for granted.

Unfortunately, your "nice" customers can absolutely kill your business. They're so nice that they never complain – so you assume everything is okay. Eventually, many of those nice customers become ex-customers.

In fact, studies show only four percent of your customers will take time to complain. They assume nothing will change anyway, so who needs the hassle? Sometimes your nice customers will consider raising an issue so they'll feel better, but it's easier to just leave quietly. Again, who needs the hassle? These customers don't bother to invest the energy in complaining because they know they're never coming back – and can you blame them?

So, how can you measure and monitor your customer connections?

Absolutely, positively connected!

Many organizations measure the percentage of satisfied customers. Most of these organizations are happy with 95 percent customer satisfaction.

At FedEx, 95 percent wasn't good enough, and neither was 99 percent. In the late 1980s, the company abandoned its measurement of on-time deliveries and replaced it with an index that described how its performance was viewed by customers. FedEx identified, weighed and monitored every factor that could go wrong in its connection with customers.

Fred Smith, CEO of FedEx, called these potential customer disconnections the "Hierarchy of Horrors." His philosophy? While all customer disconnections are bad, the worst ones need to be monitored and addressed in accordance with the severity of the disconnection.

For instance, a package delivered at 10:32 a.m. was a service failure because it did not meet the commitment time of 10:30 a.m. Any package delivered late was a service failure, but a delivery that was late by minutes was not as damaging to the customer as a delivery that was late by a day or more – that was a service disaster.

To measure and monitor their service connection, FedEx created the Service Quality Indicator (SQI) to identify each type of service failure, and then assigned a value to each one based on its impact on customer satisfaction. For example, the three most severe service failures (damaged packages, lost packages and missed pickups) were assigned a value of 10 in the SQI, while less serious problems were weighted either 5 or 1.

Every day, the SQI was monitored and service adjustments quickly made. Most adjustments were to the system and didn't involve people. However, any time performance standards were not met, the specific employee, station or department was identified, held accountable and was responsible for rapid improvement.

The result? A year after introducing the SQI, service failures were down 11 percent while package volume was up 20 percent! Thanks to the SQI and its resulting service improvements, in 1990 FedEx became the first service company to win the Malcolm Baldrige National Quality Award.

FedEx is considered one of the most reliable companies in its industry because it doesn't measure the service connection by its own internal standards – it defines and measures it from the customer's perspective.

Every organization can duplicate the FedEx model of the customer connection by following these key steps:

1. Identify your "Hierarchy of Horrors." What are the worst things that can happen in your customer interactions?

2. Develop a weighting system to bring attention to the service connections that create the most customer dissatisfaction. .

3. Implement the necessary tools to track and monitor your service connection performance.

4. Take the necessary steps to eliminate the service connection failures.

The reason FedEx is so focused on customer satisfaction is because it knows that it takes at least a dozen positive service experiences with a customer to make up for just one bad one – that's a 12:1 ratio!

If you ignore a disconnected customer, he or she will talk about the unpleasant experience – and talk about it, and talk about it some more! I'm sure all of us have heard plenty of customer-service horror stories from our friends and family. If you're nodding your head in agreement right now, you've just proved my next point: Angry customers always tell others about their bad experiences (their stories sometimes taking on lives of their own), and angry customers never forget.

The good news, though, is that most of the people who complain will do business with you again if you listen to them and personally address their complaint, quickly and efficiently. In fact, opportunities to win loyal customers are sometimes cleverly disguised as a customer complaint. If you address your customer's issues quickly and efficiently, your customer will reward you with their loyalty.

Remember: Everything counts when it comes to connecting with customers and earning a customer's loyalty. The customer focus conductor begins when the customer calls on the phone, enters your web site, or walks in the door – and it never ends!

Make the customer focus conductor a positive experience

Most customers don't expect you to do the impossible. They're not expecting miracles – they just want you to follow through and do what you promise.

While you're trying to make a connection with a customer, you may need to work doubly hard to maintain an intense customer focus that keeps you at least one step ahead of them, anticipating their needs, so that you can quickly provide them with a product that they don't even know they need.

Circus conductor

At Cirque du Soleil headquarters in Montreal, Quebec, every office looks out into the area where performers train and perfect their acts. This way every employee can see the organization's product in development.

Founded in 1984 by two street performers, *Cirque du Soleil* is a modern circus that emphasizes human performance, colorful costumes, a mixture of musical styles and an imaginary language that, strangely, is understood everywhere in the world.

By any measure, *Cirque du Soleil* is an entertainment juggernaut, selling about 7 million tickets annually that generate an estimated revenue of more than $600 million. Performances are booked three years in advance. In addition, Cirque has spun off several businesses and touring performance companies. The global impact of its brand, according to Interbrand, ranks ahead of McDonald's, Microsoft and Disney.

Cirque's success is the result of its laser-sharp focus on adult customers who are willing to pay $100 or more for a performance.

To ensure those customers see performances they'll never forget, the company hires the very best talent in the industry and every year plows more than 70 percent of its profits back into increasingly innovative projects. Its investments in people and future productions are made with the intention of delivering spectacular shows that customers will rave about long after the performance is over.

Being the very best
The reward for being the very best, as opposed to being average, is heavily skewed. People like to work for the best, buy from the best and deal with the best…in almost everything in our society. The best-selling books sell millions more copies than the average book. The best movies generate millions more dollars than the average. In almost every situation, the best in any industry is rewarded disproportionately to the average in that industry. Winners win because customers love a winner.

Customers will flock to winners.

The rewards for being the best customer-focused organization in your industry are enormous. Energy is created when customers flock to the winners. It is our choice to provide an atmosphere where our employees choose to deliver impeccable service that separates your organization from the average.

Customer Focus Conductor Summary
It's crucial to focus on your customers' needs, connect with them, and keep them happy. Customers want a connection with those they do business with – even the finest product will not keep them coming back if they don't feel a connection.

An unhappy customer who defects will tell an average of 16 people why he was dissatisfied with your service. The new customer might tell an average of two people why he is satisfied — if you're lucky. Unhappy customers also create unhappy employees — who wants to listen to customers complain all day?

Unhappy customers sap energy from your organization. But keeping a laser-sharp customer focus will generate day-to-day energy and sustain energy as your business grows.

CUSTOMER FOCUS CONDUCTOR

Having a strong connection with your customers energizes the entire organization. If your customers are unhappy, you will eventually end up with unhappy employees, too.

+ Happy customers energize employees.

+ Dissatisfied customers and dissatisfied employees become ill-willed ambassadors for your organization.

+ If you take care of your people, they will take care of your customers.

+ Opportunities to win loyal customers are sometimes cleverly disguised as a customer complaint.

+ Angry customers have elephant-like memories — they never forget!

CHAPTER EIGHT

THE INTEGRITY CONDUCTOR

Anyone who doesn't take truth seriously in small matters cannot be trusted in large ones either.

– Albert Einstein

Integrity is the cornerstone of leadership. In our Leadership Energy equation, you can think of integrity as the master switch that controls every other part of the leadership energy equation. If your organization's leadership lacks integrity, the energy will simply stop flowing through the organization. But when integrity is intact, all the parts of the equation will work.

One of the toughest things for a leader to figure out is, "What's the truth?" Many times the truth is camouflaged by politics, personal agendas, or even a sincere, intense desire to want something else to be the truth.

Leaders who search for the truth possess one of the most respected virtues in all of life – integrity. If you are truly a person who searches for the truth, regardless of politics and personal agendas, you are fast becoming a unique and valued person.

> *Weakness of attitude becomes weakness of character.*
>
> – Albert Einstein

What Is Integrity?

The dictionary says integrity is the rigid adherence to a code of behavior that can be measured only by a person's actions. Your spouse may say integrity is total commitment and loyalty. Your team may say integrity is doing what you say you'll do. Your investors may define integrity as finding no surprises in your financials. Your friends probably say it is just being who you are.

To me, integrity means never being ashamed of your reflection. If you can look in the mirror every day without regret, your integrity is in check.

Regardless of its definition and who describes it, integrity is a byproduct of trust, which in turn is a byproduct of truth and honesty. A deficit in trust can potentially cost your organization millions of dollars in sales and profits. When people lose faith and trust in their leaders, everything else goes with it: productivity, job satisfaction, morale and pride. Loss of trust will completely sap the energy from the organization, and it's unlikely that the energy can ever be restored.

Trust Matters!

It's said that people routinely question the truth of about 50 percent of everything they read.

Why? Because experience has taught them how often they encounter exaggerations, white lies and outright untruths. Almost every day, and in every type of situation, they see a trail of broken promises, unmet commitments and overstated facts. They're starting to wonder who they can believe these days. Can they believe you?

Honesty, not technique, is the secret to good communications. You may have the technique, but if you don't keep your promises and take care of business, all the technique in the world won't make you a good communicator. Trust comes before technique.

Working with people in organizations is much like being in a marriage. Honesty and trust are the basic foundation for any successful relationship – between colleagues, with customers, or among friends. Relationships are built and sustained on trust. If the trust is broken, some relationships cannot be mended.

Marianne M. Jennings is a professor of legal and ethical studies in business at Arizona State University. In a recent article, she writes, "There is a circle of trust in the capitalistic economy, and to the extent that the conductor of trust is lost, there will be a breakdown in the free enterprise system that affords opportunity for individual achievement." Powerful words with an even more powerful message: Without trust, entire economies and systems can fail. There is no energy without trust.

Jennings provides a compelling illustration of the power of honesty:

"Professor Frank Shipper, a management expert at Salisbury State University in Maryland, explored the questions of why some managers had survived the countless corporate downsizings over the past decade. These were managers who had not suffered a corporate loss of employment while many of their peers in management were left unemployed for spans of up to a year.

"Professor Shipper found two very important characteristics about these managers. First, this was a diverse group of people that included women and men of various ages, different races, and varying styles of management. Second, both the managers themselves and their employees used one common descriptive adjective: honest.

"These managers were honest in all aspects of their work. They gave credit to their employees for ideas taken forward to senior executives and explained to them new rules, new strategies, and policy or procedural changes with candor. The business urban legends of politicking, networking, and climbing the ladder of success on the backs of others were foreign to these managers.

"These managers understood not just being honest, but also the importance of the gospel principles of kindness and fairness. They were successful because of these qualities, not despite them. Their employment security resulted from a simple devotion to basic commandments of honesty."

Be prepared to be honest
Business practices are more exposed today than at any time in history. Because so many once-lauded organizations were found to

be morally destitute in the early part of this decade, the Sarbanes-Oxley legislation and other measures make it imperative for organizations and individuals to be honest. Period.

In the movie, *Chalk*, a semi-documentary about the trials and tribulations of high-school teachers, they are filmed at a meeting where they're asked penetrating questions, such as: "How many of you have taken home a stapler that belonged to the school? How many have used a ream of paper to make fliers for your personal weekend garage sales? How many of you have borrowed money from your organizational fundraiser to buy a round of beer on Friday afternoon?"

Sadly, by the time all the questions had been asked, many teachers were guiltily looking at their feet.

Staplers and paper seem like such small things, but personal honesty is the basis of the corporate image. If Cynthia laughs about charging a personal dinner on the corporate credit card, then what will her customer think about the integrity of that business?

Improper charges on expense reports are symptomatic of a bigger problem with ethics. And if a company's ethics are questionable, depletion of its energy can't be far behind.

After the demise of Enron and WorldCom, organizations that understood the importance of integrity began developing a culture that demands honesty and ethical behavior, and punishes those who fall short of the standard.

When organizations have zero tolerance for dishonesty or unethical behavior, their brands and their images survive. These companies will ultimately win competitive battles because they know without a doubt who they are, what they are, and where they are headed.

Creating a Culture of Integrity

There are four pillars that you can uphold to create a culture of integrity. Failure to adhere to any of the four will destroy confidence and trust in your leadership:

1. *Keep your promises and promise only what you can deliver.* It may sound simple, but many leaders make the mistake of over-committing or committing to something beyond their control. Living up to your commitments is one of the principal ways your integrity is judged.

2. *Stand up and speak out for what you believe.* Your integrity begins when you speak out about what you believe. What are your core values? What's so important that it will never be compromised for any reason?

   Never leave people guessing about how you feel or where you stand. Understand exactly what you believe and communicate those beliefs without hesitation. If your beliefs and values are integrity based, they will never change.

3. *Err on the side of fairness.* In a gray area, err on the side of fairness. What you do is being closely watched by your team, and their judgments are based on their perception of what they observe. It may not be fair, but you have to manage your people's perceptions – not all decisions are black or white. Err on the side of your team. Swallowing your pride is a small price to pay to retain or gain their trust in you.

4. *Live what you teach.* People listen to what you say and watch the way you deliver the message, but they react to what they see you do. You can't fake what you teach. Walk your talk! The ultimate test of your integrity is whether you do what you said you'd do. Your word and your commitment are judged every time you commit to something – regardless of how insignificant you consider the commitment. When your integrity is sacrificed for any reason, recovering it won't be easy.

When you fail to treasure the truthful and forthright, you will gradually find yourself surrounded by flattering fools who conceal truths for their convenience and yours. When the stakes for saying and hearing the truth are too high, one lives a life of deceit.

Integrity Conductor Summary

Business is personal. People commit themselves to other people more than to an organization. If people don't trust the messenger, they won't buy into the message. Leadership begins with the leader's integrity. Without integrity, you can't develop trust, and without trust, nothing else really matters. Trust and honesty are the keys to integrity.

Integrity is not just being fiscally trustworthy or handling issues in an exemplary and truthful fashion. Integrity is the commitment to do what is right regardless of the circumstance. If your organization lacks integrity, the energy will stop flowing and all the other energy conductors will cease to matter.

THE INTEGRITY CONDUCTOR

✦ One of the toughest things for a leader to figure out is "What is the truth?"

✦ If you are a person who searches for the truth – regardless of politics or personal agenda – you are a unique and valued person.

✦ Integrity is never being ashamed of your reflection.

✦ There can be no positive energy without trust.

✦ The ultimate test of integrity is whether you do what you said you would do.

Part Three:

Optimizing Energy Resources

The Leader's Impact on Energy

The Final Word

CHAPTER NINE

THE LEADER'S IMPACT ON ENERGY

In order to be an immaculate member of a flock of sheep,
one must above all be a sheep oneself.

– Albert Einstein

Three hundred years ago, Alexander the Great led his troops across a hot and desolate plain. After 11 days of a grueling advance, he and all the soldiers were near death from thirst. They pressed on, however, into the 12th day.

At midday, two of his scouts brought Alexander what little water they had been able to find. It hardly filled a cup. His troops stood back and watched – expecting him to drink. Instead, he poured the water into the hot sand. Without saying a word, Alexander energized his followers by providing the only things he had to give at that moment: example and inspiration.

The multiplier to Leadership Energy is **YOU**. YOU are the secret power that your organization has been waiting for. YOU have tremendous influence to bring about change in your organization – to harness and release its energy, to conduct and focus that energy, and to multiply it throughout the entire organization.

But where do you even begin? How do you start re-energizing your team?

It sounds simple, but you can begin by being enthusiastic – even when you don't feel like it. If you're enthusiastic, those around you will be, too. Enthusiasm multiplies energy to produce positive results!

Johnny Harrell owned a service station back in the days when service was still a part of filling your gas tank. Johnny came back from a leadership conference all fired up. He'd been told that enthusiasm alone would produce better results in business. So he called his employees together and declared, "This week we're going to conduct an experiment in enthusiasm. I want you to check the oil filter of everyone who drives in here. I want you to make an enthusiastic presentation to them about what a new oil filter can do for them if they need it."

The men went to work and carried out Johnny's instructions. At the end of the week, he checked his records to see if their enthusiastic oil-filter presentations had made any difference. And guess what? They'd sold 700 percent more oil filters than in the previous best week *in 15 years.*

What was the difference? His business was still in the same location with the same men offering the same thing. The difference was *enthusiasm.* Sincere enthusiasm creates energy and produces positive results even when nothing else changes. Try it!

Physical Energy Creates Lifestyle Energy

Maybe knowing how critical you are to your organization seems a little bit overwhelming. If you're the one responsible for constantly energizing everyone else, how do you energize YOU?

It may sound obvious, but if you're lacking physical energy, you'll find it tough to increase any other kind of energy. It's difficult to be energetic and enthusiastic when you're physically out of shape. I know you've heard this before, but it's a simple truth – increasing your physical energy level may require lifestyle changes.

Seven years ago, I underwent quadruple bypass heart surgery. Although it wasn't much fun, my heart disease was a wakeup call that forced me to change my lifestyle. The results have been positive, and I've improved my health and increased my energy.

If you need to make lifestyle changes, start now. Don't wait until you're lying on a gurney awaiting surgery. Take some time to evaluate: Are you getting enough rest? What about your exercise schedule – or does one even exist? Does your diet consist mainly of quick lunches and fast food? Are you eating more meat and potatoes than fruits and vegetables?

You can also increase your personal energy by decreasing your liquor tab. Any physician will tell you that alcohol consumption actually saps your energy. You may feel a momentary buzz after a couple of cocktails or during that third glass of wine, but don't confuse that with energy – it's just the alcohol talking. Continued alcohol consumption will drain your energy.

The bottom line: If you want to increase your organization's energy, start by increasing your own energy first. Eat a healthy diet, get enough sleep, engage in regular stress-reducing exercise, and spend some time every day focusing on your spiritual self. Your body and your mind will thank you – and reward you with more stamina.

Continuous Improvement Creates Energy

The most successful leaders are those who continue to learn and improve every day. Quite simply, leaders who are not committed to personal improvement are doomed to fail. Complacency is the root of mediocrity.

The most successful leaders energize themselves by reading about successful people. They discover that others have faced challenges similar to their own and have prospered by working through them. Choose a regular time and place to read, then *do* it. Read. It's impossible to energize your organization if you don't take the time to energize yourself.

> *Education is what remains after one has forgotten everything he learned in school.*
>
> – Albert Einstein

Start off by reading a book a month – it'll change your life. More than 20 years ago, I started reading at least a book a month, and I soon discovered that the more you learn, the more you earn. Discover it for yourself.

There are hundreds of books to help you become more productive, yet most people read less than one book a year. If you prefer a high-tech approach, download audio books or motivational Podcasts that you can plug into during a flight. Take advantage of technology to educate and motivate yourself professionally, personally and spiritually, and you'll take control of your life!

Whatever your profession, choose to be the best. By reading for just ten minutes a day, you can finish a book in a month and join the top one percent in the nation in your profession.

In addition, place on your nightstand a book of famous quotations, and every morning put a positive thought in your head before you roll out of bed. You could read my collection, *David Cottrell's Collection of Favorite Quotations*, or anyone else's. There are plenty of good ones around. If you start your day with a positive thought, you'll make a positive difference.

Another choice you can make to gain energy through knowledge is to use your commute time wisely. The average person spends more than 500 hours each year commuting – the equivalent of more than 12 forty-hour weeks! Convert some of that time to energizing yourself and preparing for the workday. The more energized you are during your drive time, the better prepared you will be to face the challenges of your day.

In today's business world, with the explosion of information and technology, continuing education is no longer an option for success – it's a necessity! A PhD earned today is obsolete within five years because information and theories are changing so rapidly. Keep yourself informed, and you'll keep up with changes.

Values Create Energy

Every path in business involves difficult choices that may not be clearly right or wrong, or choices that challenge our faith, commitment, and desire to keep going.

The key to increasing your energy and making the best decisions is to understand your values. What's the one thing that you will not compromise under any circumstances? Until you know your number one value, you cannot commit to numbers two, three or four.

Your values create your energy to lead. Once you identify your values, your choices are easier. But compromising your values will instantly drain energy from you and your team.

Values help us be strong in our commitments and consistent in meeting our challenges. The following tips will help:

1. **Ensure your job matches your values.**

   Many people occupy jobs that are wrong for them, and they're discontented because their professional lives conflict with their values. If you're in that situation, you're guaranteed to be miserable and to make everyone around you miserable, too.

   You probably know some very intelligent, very successful but very unhappy people who face a clash of values, day in and day out. Maybe their jobs require constant time away from their families. The money is great, but their families mean much more.

   These people will never reach their potential until their values align with their daily lives. You cannot be happy at work if you constantly think your work is forcing you to compromise your values.

   "In order to succeed," the late Will Rogers said, "you must know what you are doing, like what you are doing and believe in what you are doing." A passion for your job will create energy and focus for you to lead others. If you're not comfortable telling others what you do, you're likely in the wrong job.

2. Set personal goals.

You cannot fulfill any dream without first understanding your purpose. It's been said that less than five percent of people have personal goals they're actually working to accomplish. Your personal goals are the rudder for your life; they steer you in the right direction. You will not achieve your purpose if you cannot define what you are trying to accomplish.

✦ First, identify your personal goals and write them down. Second, set a monthly goal and establish what actions are needed to accomplish that goal. Do this for two months, and you'll see more satisfaction at work and at home.

✦ Develop an accountability group. Pick one or two ambitious, fun, positive people whom you admire, and meet with them once a week just to talk. This accountability group will help you keep your sanity when you need to talk things out. It's important to have a group to relate to and be yourself with. Pick a group, find the time, choose the place, and lift each other's spirits.

✦ Mentor others. Everyone needs encouragement from time to time. Make the effort to encourage others, and you'll receive encouragement in return. Several years ago, a survey asked people whether they had a mentor, and 86 percent of respondents said no. Eighty-six percent! People make better decisions when they have a mentor to follow, so it's a good business decision to become a mentor. However, as the mentor, you will receive the greatest return on investment! You will become what you teach, and you will become accountable for your teaching. Mentoring others will pay dividends many times over.

✦ Keep your sense of humor. When you stop laughing at yourself, you're taking yourself too seriously. Enjoy the different personalities on your team and don't be afraid to admit mistakes or laugh at yourself. Job satisfaction requires a good sense of humor. People who can laugh at life are healthier, happier and more energized. Use your sense of humor to make life fun!

> *It is really a puzzle what drives one*
> *to take one's work so devilishly seriously.*
>
> – Albert Einstein

3. Hang in there long enough to win!

Without a doubt, there are some who give up too soon – just before they turn the corner to success. Successful people keep moving even when they are scared and have made mistakes.

The following story illustrates what happens to many on the road to success:

A man meets a guru in the road and asks, "Which way is success?"

The bearded sage doesn't speak, but points to the left.

The man, thrilled by the prospect of quick and easy success, rushes off. Suddenly, there's a loud *SPLAT!*

Eventually the man limps back, tattered and stunned, assuming he took a wrong turn. So he repeats his question to the guru, who again points silently in the same direction.

The man obediently walks off, and this time there's a deafening *SPLAAAAT!*

When the man crawls back, he is bloody, broken and irate. "I asked you which way to success!" he screams at the guru. "I followed your direction, but all I got was splatted – twice! No more pointing! Talk!"

Only then does the guru speak, very quietly. "Success is that way. Just a little past splat."

Many of us would be tempted to give up after the first *SPLAT!* But we must develop the courage and resolve to hang in there, through several rounds of splatting, if necessary! If you persevere and work through the issues, you can and will make a difference!

> *Great spirits have always encountered violent opposition from mediocre minds.*
>
> – Albert Einstein

THE LEADER'S IMPACT ON ENERGY

✦ Enthusiasm creates energy and produces positive results even when nothing else changes.

✦ If you want to increase your organization's energy, start by increasing your own energy.

✦ Complacency is the root of mediocrity.

✦ Whatever your profession, choose to be the best.

CHAPTER TEN

THE FINAL WORD

Anyone who has never made a mistake has never tried anything new.

– Albert Einstein

Albert Einstein's ground-breaking formula, $E=mc^2$, was derived when Einstein dared to challenge accepted scientific principles that had not changed since the time of Newton, 200 years before. Einstein's theory radically changed human understanding of the universe and led to significant developments that changed history.

Energy is essential to success in organizations today. If there is no excitement, no enthusiasm and no passion, there is no catalyst for achievement.

The good news is that your organization is an incredible reservoir of energy just waiting to be released. And that is the task of the leader – to find a way to tap into that energy, conduct it and multiply it throughout the organization.

But in taking on that task, it's important to remember the following:

- *Leaders get what they do.* You are the role model that your team is following. People follow people more so than value statements, mission statements, memos, and e-mails. You must continually, clearly and concisely communicate an exciting, authentic and enthusiastic vision for your people to buy into and treat as their own.

- *The more involved leaders are, the better their decisions.* To lead your people, you must know your people and involve them in your decisions. Most of the time your team is collectively better informed than you − all you have to do is ask them the right questions, and you'll find that they have the right answers.

- *Get the right people in the right jobs.* Nothing is more important to the energy of an organization than having the right people on the team.

You are the ultimate energizer. Challenge yourself. Dig deep into the role of a leader. Read all that you can about leadership and become a life-long learner. Strive to keep your knowledge fresh and your attitude positive. Develop and apply new skills to help accelerate your growth.

May life's journey bring you energy, success and prosperity!

About the Author

David Cottrell, president and CEO of CornerStone Leadership Institute, is an internationally known leadership educator and speaker. His business experience includes leadership positions with Xerox and FedEx.

He is the author of more than 20 books, including *Monday Morning Leadership; Monday Morning Mentoring; Monday Morning Choices; Listen Up, Leader;* and *The Next Level: Leadership Beyond the Status Quo.*

David is a thought-provoking and electrifying professional speaker. He has presented his leadership message to over 250,000 managers worldwide. His powerful wisdom and insights on leadership have made him a highly sought-after keynote speaker and seminar leader.

David can be reached at www.**CornerStoneLeadership**.com

Bring *Leadership Energy* to Your Organization

Leadership Energy **PowerPoint® Presentation**
Introduce and reinforce *Leadership Energy* to your organization with this complete and cost-effective companion presentation piece. All of the main concepts and ideas in the book are reinforced in this professionally produced, downloadable PowerPoint presentation with facilitator guide and notes. Use the presentation for kick-off meetings, training sessions or as a follow-up development tool. $99.95

Keynote Presentation
Invite David Cottrell to deliver the *Leadership Energy* message and inspire your team. This presentation will set a solid foundation for improving your organization's success. For more information, contact David Cottrell at www.CornerStoneLeadership.com.

The *Leadership Energy* Workshop
Facilitated by a certified CornerStone Leadership instructor, this three- or six-hour workshop will reinforce the principles of *Leadership Energy.*

For additional information, call 1-888-789-5323 or visit www.CornerStoneLeadership.com.

Accelerate Powerful Leadership Package
$199⁹⁵

☑ **YES! Please send me extra copies of *Leadership Energy***
1-30 copies $14.95   31-99 copies $13.95   100+ copies $12.95

Leadership Energy	_____ copies X _____	= $ _____
Leadership Energy PowerPoint™	_____ copies X $99.95	= $ _____

Accelerate Powerful Leadership Resources

Accelerate Powerful Leadership Package _____ pack(s) X $199.95   = $ _____
(Includes one each of all items pictured
on page 110.)

Other Books

_____	_____ copies X _____	= $ _____
_____	_____ copies X _____	= $ _____
_____	_____ copies X _____	= $ _____
_____	_____ copies X _____	= $ _____
	Shipping & Handling	$ _____
	Subtotal	$ _____
	Sales Tax (8.25%-TX Only)	$ _____
	Total (U.S. Dollars Only)	**$ _____**

Shipping and Handling Charges

Total $ Amount	Up to $49	$50-$99	$100-$249	$250-$1199	$1200-$2999	$3000+
Charge	$7	$9	$16	$30	$80	$125

Name _____ Job Title_____

Organization _____ Phone_____

Shipping Address _____ Fax _____

Billing Address_____E-mail _____
(required when ordering PowerPoint® Presentation)

City_____ State _____ ZIP_____

❑ Please invoice (Orders over $200) Purchase Order Number (if applicable)_____

Charge Your Order: ❑ MasterCard   ❑ Visa   ❑ American Express

Credit Card Number _____ Exp. Date_____

Signature _____

❑ Check Enclosed (Payable to: CornerStone Leadership)

Fax	**Mail**	**Phone**
972.274.2884	P.O. Box 764087	888.789.5323
	Dallas, TX 75376	

115887

Thank you for reading *Leadership Energy*.
We hope it has assisted you in your quest for
personal and professional growth.

To help you facilitate teaching these concepts to your team,
a PowerPoint® slide presentation is available at
www.CornerStoneLeadership.com

Best wishes for your continued success.

CornerStone
Leadership Institute
www.CornerStoneLeadership.com

Start a crusade in your organization –
have the courage to learn, the vision to lead,
and the passion to share.